THE
DUTIES
OF SERVANTS

This guide was originally published in 1894.
This new edition contains illustrations and photographs
of Victorian household objects from private collections.

THE DUTIES OF SERVANTS

A PRACTICAL GUIDE to
The Routine of Domestic Service

Copper Beech Publishing

This edition published by Copper Beech Publishing Ltd
This edition © copyright
Copper Beech Publishing Ltd

ISBN 0 9516295 9 X

Copper Beech Publishing Ltd
P O Box 159, East Grinstead,
Sussex, RH19 4FS England

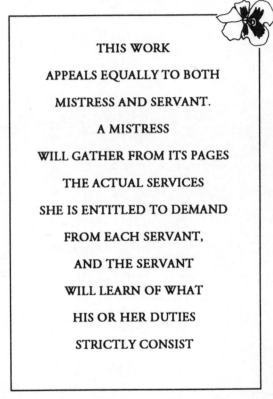

THIS WORK

APPEALS EQUALLY TO BOTH

MISTRESS AND SERVANT.

A MISTRESS

WILL GATHER FROM ITS PAGES

THE ACTUAL SERVICES

SHE IS ENTITLED TO DEMAND

FROM EACH SERVANT,

AND THE SERVANT

WILL LEARN OF WHAT

HIS OR HER DUTIES

STRICTLY CONSIST

ENGAGING AND DISMISSING SERVANTS

The important duty of engaging and dismissing servants devolves upon various individuals according to the scale on which each household is regulated.

In large establishments the house-steward engages and dismisses both the men and women servants. Where there is no house-steward at the head of a household, the housekeeper engages and dismisses the female servants; and the butler the indoor men-servants, but in all cases a master and mistress of a house engage their own personal attendants, viz., the valet, ladies'-maids, and nurse. Where a house-steward is not kept, the master of the house engages the coachman.

Where a housekeeper is not kept the mistress of a house engages the women-servants, the master of the house engages the butler and footmen, unless the butler is an old and trustworthy servant, in which case engaging and dismissing the footmen is left in his hands.

In households of smaller dimensions the master of the house engages and dismisses the men-servants, and the mistress of the house the women-servants. Where one man-servant is kept, the mistress of the house not unfrequently engages him.

In the stable department the master of the house engages and dismisses the coachman and the grooms. It is only when a coachman is an old and trusted servant that he is deputed to engage the grooms and stable helpers.

In engaging servants a personal character is very much insisted upon, and it offers many advantages, as far more can be said in an interview than can be expressed by letter; questions can be asked and answered, and particulars given, which do away with the necessity of taking a servant for a month on trial.

When it is not possible to obtain a personal character on the ground of distance, state of health, or other equally good reasons, a written character should always be supplemented by some indirect personal knowledge, to avoid the possibility of imposture being attempted. It is often that the minor points in a servant's character are of paramount importance in the eyes of a mistress, and ladies are always more inclined to express their opinion with greater freedom in an interview then by letter.

In engaging servants it is advisable to put the following leading questions:-

"*With whom have you been living?*" or "*In what family have you been living?*" "*How long were you with them?*" or "*Have you been there long?*" "*What was the reason of your leaving?*" "*What is your age?*" "*Is your health good?*" "*Are you an early riser?*" "*What wages have you been receiving?*" After these questions, those relating to the duties appertaining to the situation applied for are entered upon. If the applicant is a cook, questions such as the following would be useful. "*Are you a professed cook?*" "*Have you been in the habit of sending up large dinners?*" "*How many were there in family in your last place?*" and "*How many servants had you to cook for?*" "*I suppose you understand making smart sweets and entrées?*" and so on, which questions will elicit a full explanation of what the cook can or cannot do.

The question of per-centage from the trades people with whom the family deals is one that a mistress when engaging a cook should be explicit upon and clearly make it understood that it is not allowed under pain of dismissal, if such is the rule of the house; and heads of houses who wish to keep the household expenses within reasonable limits are very firm upon this point.

Many cooks are so independent that they decline situations where per-centage is not allowed, and many also object to taking a situation where they are not permitted to order everything that is required for consumption in the house, or where the mistress ventures upon giving orders to the tradespeople herself. Therefore, if a mistress does not intend placing such power in the hands of her cook, she should make it distinctly understood at the time of engaging her, as those mistresses who prefer saving themselves trouble and to whom the practice of economy is not a consideration, are in the habit of allowing the cook to order everything required in the kitchen, even to choosing and changing the tradespeople of whom the things are ordered. In the every-day consumption of a household the cook must necessarily give orders.

It rests with mistresses to make their own rules as to the amount of liberty they allow their servants, and this should be done when engaging them, to avoid any future misunderstanding. Many masters and mistresses, providing the men-servants are in by half-past ten or eleven, do not object to their going out when dinner is over. Any rule or rules which a mistress of a house may think proper to make, such as deducting the cost of breakages from wages, or restrictions as to personal attire, should be mentioned at the time of engaging a servant, as it is unfair to impose rules upon servants who have taken a situation in ignorance of them.

The rule as to whether servants may receive visits from male acquaintances is a very important one, and the prohibition of such should be clearly expressed. In well-ordered households the visits of male acquaintances, commonly called "followers," are strictly forbidden; and all mistresses desirous of maintaining anything like order in their households, rigidly enforce the observance of this regulation. In large establishments male visitors to the women servants are not in any way permitted; but in small households the visits of male acquaintances are looked upon as a privilege, the resisting which is a continual source of annoyance to a mistress. The order, method, and regularity that reigns in large establishments could with advantage and profit be maintained in smaller households, where an undue amount of laxness too often prevails.

Bettering themselves: in large establishments the inducement offered to the under servants in the way of "*bettering themselves*," as it is termed, is the promotion which takes place in their ranks, the scullery-maid is advanced to be kitchen-maid, the third house-maid to be second house-maid; the second footman to be first footman, and so on; in small households where there is no room for such promotion, a usual and satisfactory plan is to engage servants on the promise of a rise in their wages every succeeding year. Mistresses who can only afford to give a certain sum, object to this arrangement on the ground that, at the end of two, three, or five years, the wages they were giving their servants would be higher than their incomes justified, and are often put to the constant inconvenience of losing a good servant and perhaps gaining an inexperienced one.

When a servant gives notice to leave, a mistress should never exhibit any displeasure or vexation she may feel on the subject, but calmly inquire the reason of the determination. If it is merely a question of wages and she has the power and inclination to comply with the required advance, she at once agrees to it, by giving a servant an opportunity of stating her reasons for leaving; the chance is afforded of anything radically wrong in the establishment being made known to the mistress of it; but when a servant is "making a change" from purely personal reasons or from grievance that a mistress cannot attempt to redress.

A master or mistress can either give a servant a month's notice or a month's wages in lieu of notice, or can dismiss them before the month's notice has expired by paying the moiety of the unexpired month's notice.

A servant can be dismissed without notice for impropriety of conduct, insobriety, dishonesty, or disobedience, but cannot be dismissed for a threat of disobedience made to a fellow-servant and not put into execution.

A master and mistress are not compelled by law to give a servant a character even though they may have received one with a servant, unless at the time of engaging a servant an agreement is made to do so.

A servant cannot claim a month's board wages when receiving a month's wages in lieu of notice.

SERVANTS' WAGES OR TABLE OF INCOME.

Per Year.			Per Month.			Per Week.			Per Day.		
£	s.	d.	£	s.	d.	£	s.	d.	£	s.	d.
5	0	0	0	8	4	0	1	11	0	0	3¼
5	5	0	0	8	9	0	2	0¼	0	0	3½
5	10	0	0	9	2	0	2	1½	0	0	3½
6	0	0	0	10	0	0	2	3¾	0	0	4
6	6	0	0	10	6	0	2	5	0	0	4¼
6	10	0	0	10	10	0	2	6	0	0	4¼
7	0	0	0	11	8	0	2	8¼	0	0	4½
7	7	0	0	12	3	0	2	10	0	0	4¾
7	10	0	0	12	6	0	2	10½	0	0	5
8	0	0	0	13	4	0	3	1	0	0	5¼
8	8	0	0	14	0	0	3	2¾	0	0	5½
8	10	0	0	14	2	0	3	3¼	0	0	5½
9	0	0	0	15	0	0	3	5½	0	0	6
9	9	0	0	15	9	0	3	7½	0	0	6¼
10	0	0	0	16	8	0	3	10¼	0	0	6½
10	10	0	0	17	6	0	4	0½	0	0	7
11	0	0	0	18	4	0	4	2¾	0	0	7¼
11	11	0	0	19	3	0	4	5¼	0	0	7½
12	0	0	1	0	0	0	4	7½	0	0	8
12	12	0	1	1	0	0	4	10¼	0	0	8¼
13	0	0	1	1	8	0	5	0	0	0	8½
13	13	0	1	2	9	0	5	3	0	0	9
14	0	0	1	3	4	0	5	4½	0	0	9¼
14	14	0	1	4	6	0	5	7¾	0	0	9¾
15	0	0	1	5	0	0	5	9¼	0	0	9¾
15	15	0	1	6	3	0	6	0¾	0	0	10¼
16	0	0	1	6	8	0	6	1¾	0	0	10½
16	16	0	1	8	0	0	6	5½	0	0	11
17	0	0	1	8	4	0	6	6½	0	0	11¼
17	17	0	1	9	9	0	6	10½	0	0	11¾
18	0	0	1	10	0	0	6	11	0	0	11¾

If the sum be guineas instead of pounds, add one penny to each month, or one farthing to each week.

A TARIFF OF SERVANTS' WAGES

The tariff of wages paid to domestic servants fluctuates very considerably, and is influenced in a great measure by the position of a master and mistress, and by the experience of the servant.

Higher wages are given in town than in the country, and experienced servants ask higher wages than do inexperienced ones.

The scale of wages may be said to commence with the house-steward.

A **house-steward** receives £50 to £80 per annum, according to the responsibilities of his office.

A **groom of the chambers** receives £40 to £50 per annum.

A **butler** receives £50 to £80 per annum.

A **valet** receives £30 to £50 per annum.

The wages of a **man cook** varies from £100 and upwards; some men cooks receive as much as £150, besides perquisites.

Neither of these servants wear livery, and they find themselves in clothes.

An **under-butler** or **head footman** receives £28 to £32, and two to three suits of livery per year.

The **under-footmen** receive £14 to £20, and upwards.

A **coachman** receives £25 to £60, and two suits of livery.

A **second coachman** receives £20 to £35, and two suits of livery.

A **head-groom** receives £18 to £25 per annum, and two suits of livery.

An **under-groom** £14 to £20 per annum, and two suits of livery.

A **page** receives £7 to £12 per annum, and two suits of livery.

A **steward's-room boy** and **servant's-hall boy** receive £6 to £8 per annum.

A **housekeeper** receives £30 to £70 per annum.

A **plain cook** receives £50 to £70 per annum.

A **head kitchen-maid** receives £20 to £28 per annum.

A **parlour-maid** from £16 to £24.

A **second kitchen-maid** receives £14 to £22 per annum.

In the case of only one kitchen-maid being kept, she receives from £18 to £24 per annum.

A **scullery-maid** receives £12 to £18 per annum.

A **still-room maid** receives £10 to £14 per annum.

An **upper house-maid** receives £20 to £30 per annum.

A **second house-maid** receives £14 to £20 per annum.

A **third house-maid** receives £12 to £18 per annum.

A **house-maid**, where only one is kept, also receives from £12 to £18 per annum.

A **lady's-maid** receives from £20 to £35 per annum; a young-ladies'-maid from £14 to £25 per annum.

A **head nurse** receives from £20 to £30 per annum.

An **under-nurse** receives from £14 to £18 per annum.

A **nursery-maid** receives from £10 to £14 per annum.

A **school-room maid** receives from £10 to £14 per annum.

A **head laundry-maid** receives from £18 to £24 per annum. A house parlour-maid from £15 to £20.

A **second laundry-maid** receives from £16 to £20 per annum.

A **third laundry-maid** receives from £12 to £16 per annum.

Where only one laundry-maid is kept she receives

from £18 to £25 per annum.

A **dairy-maid** receives from £14 to £20 per annum.

In some households, tea, sugar, beer, and washing are found; in others extra wages are allowed for these.

When tea and sugar are allowanced, the usual quantity allowed to each servant is, 1 lb. of tea per month, and 2 lbs. of loaf sugar, or money to this equivalent.

When beer money is given, it varies from 1s.6d. to 2s.6d. per week; in some households the under female servants are allowed but 1s. per week. For the quantity of beer allowed to each servant per day, see Chapter on "Servants' Meals."

When money for washing is allowed it varies from 1s. to 2s.6d per week.

When families are out of town the servants left in the house are put on board wages, and some families allow their servants board wages during the whole of the year, as mentioned in Chapter on "Servants' Meals."

The board wages allowed to men servants are:-

For butlers, from 14s. to 16s. per week. Footmen, 13s. to 14s. per week. And to women servants, from 12s. to 14s. per week to the upper maid servants, and from 11s. to 13s. to the under servants.

Respecting the tariff of wages paid to out-door

servants, when paid weekly - Coachmen receive from
16s. to 25s. per week, lower wages being given in the
country than in town. In addition to this they are
allowed rooms over the stables, or a cottage, rent free,
and a fire in the harness-room when required.

Grooms receive from 10s. to 18s. per week.

The liveries given to men servants depend upon
how long a family remains in town, or the amount of
company kept. Some families allow each man servant
two livery suits and a working suit per year, while
others allow three suits of livery and two working
suits in two years. In each case the livery is the
property of the master.

The other out-door servants comprise gardeners,
game-keepers, and dairy-maids.

A head gardener receives from £75 to £80 per
annum and a house rent free.

The under-gardeners from £45 to £50 per annum.

Gardeners are either paid by the week or by the
quarter.

Head game-keepers receive 35s. to 40s. per week.

Under game-keepers from 15s. to 25s. per week.

A head chauffeur receives from £3 to £4 per week
in a large establishment where three or four cars and
an assistant chauffeur are kept.

A young chauffeur mechanic receives £2 per week,
which includes board wages; or £1.10s per week and
board wages.

The board wages usually given to a chauffeur is about 12s. per week.

A chauffeur who was formerly coachman or footman receives 30s. per week.

A chauffeur is supplied with livery, consisting of coat, waistcoat, breeches and gaiters, an overcoat, cap, dust-coat and overalls for cleaning car.

The footman or groom sitting alongside the chauffeur receives a similar livery.

When servants are engaged, they are entitled to have the cost of their journey paid by their master or mistress. If they are dismissed for no actual misconduct, they are also entitled to have their return-journey paid; but if a servant gives notice, he or she is not entitled to receive return-journey money.

Game-keepers are usually allowed a cottage rent free, in addition to their wages.

SERVANTS' MEALS

Punctuality with regard to meals in the servants' hall is as imperative as with regard to those in the dining-room. In large establishments this regularity is in force, as a matter of course, but in smaller households a laxness in this particular not unfrequently exists; and this, although attributed to the cook, might, in many cases, be laid to the charge of the mistress of the house, who fails to insist that strict punctuality should be maintained.

Without early rising, there can be little or no punctuality in a household. In large establishments early rising is compulsory, but in smaller households, this early rising is too often optional, and is not sufficiently considered by mistresses in general.

Eight o'clock in summer, and half-past eight in winter is the usual breakfast hour both in the house-keeper's room and in the servants' hall. In large establishments the upper servants breakfast in the steward's room instead of in the housekeeper's room. When meals take place in the steward's room the steward's boy lays the table; when in the housekeeper's room the still-room maid does so; when in the servants' hall the servants'-hall boy, or scullery-maid.

The upper servants include the house-steward, the groom of the chambers, the butler, the housekeeper, the cook, the valet, the lady's-maid, and the nurse. It is, however, chiefly in noblemen's houses and the houses of the very wealthy that a house-steward is kept, and that the upper servants have their breakfast, tea, and supper in the steward's room; in ordinary establishments these meals take place in the house-keeper's room.

In small households consisting of three women-servants only, there is generally speaking, no house-keeper's room or servants' hall, in which case the servants have their meals in the kitchen.

Whether in the steward's-room or housekeeper's-room, it is the housekeeper's duty to pour out the tea. The cups and saucers are placed on a large tea-tray, with slop-basin, sugar-basin, milk-jug, teapot and coffee-pot. A knife and fork and plate are placed for each person; the cruet stand is set on the centre of the table, and salt-cellar at each corner.

Cold meat is given for breakfast, such as ham, meat pie, cold roast or boiled pork. When eggs are plentiful, they are given, and very frequently fried bacon. Whatever meat is given is placed opposite the butler and carved by him. In some houses rolls are given for breakfast, but when not, a loaf of bread, dry-toast, and butter in a butter-dish, are placed on the table.

In the servants' hall breakfast is arranged in a similar manner. The head housemaid or kitchen-maid pours out the tea or coffee, and the under butler or footman carves the cold meat - bacon and eggs being seldom given in the servants' hall.

Sometimes the grooms prefer beer instead of tea or coffee for breakfast.

Breakfast in the kitchen is conducted on the same principle: the cook pours out the tea and carves the cold meat.

The breakfast-things are cleared away by those whose duty it is to lay breakfast. It is also the duty of these under servants to prepare lunch at eleven o'clock in the different rooms. In large houses cold meat and beer are given for lunch; in smaller households, bread and cheese and beer.

One o'clock is the usual hour for the servants' dinner. The general rule is for the upper and under servants to sit down to table together in the servants' hall, the upper servants being the first to enter, and for the upper servants to have the sweets and bread and cheese in the housekeeper's room. The dinner-table is laid by the servants'-hall boy; it is covered with a white tablecloth, a knife and fork and tumbler are placed for each person, and a table-spoon and salt cellar at each corner; a cruet stand in the middle of the table. The hot meat and vegetables are placed upon the table; and, where there are two joints provided, they are carved by the butler and the housekeeper. The bread and jugs of beer are not placed on the table, but are helped by the footman as required.

The still-room maid lays the table in the housekeeper's room, where the upper servants adjourn to finish their dinner. The table is covered with a white table-cloth; a knife and fork, dessert-spoon, and tumbler are placed for each person. The pudding or tart, or both, are brought into the housekeeper's room by the still-room maid when the servants are seated at table, and are placed opposite the housekeeper. The still-room maid hands the plates round to those seated at table, and then returns to finish her own dinner: the bell is rung for her to bring in the cheese as soon as the sweet has been eaten.

Some ladies leave the arrangement of the servants' dinner entirely to the discretion of the cook,
and do not even inquire what servants are to have for
dinner; but in smaller households, or even in large
households, where ladies are their own housekeepers,
and where economy is practised, and where prodigal-
ity is discountenanced, ladies order the servants'
dinner at the same time that they order their own
dinner. Again, in large households both the upper
and under servants are allowed puddings every day as
a matter of course, and in some small households it is
also the rule to allow puddings for dinner, while in
others, puddings are only allowed once or twice a
week, under the mistaken idea that they add considerably to the expenses of housekeeping! Other mistresses of households adopt a medium course, and
give Yorkshire pudding, suet pudding, batter pudding, with hot joints, and sweet puddings with cold
joints. *This is the most economical plan, but servants
as a rule dislike a cold dinner, and when it can be
arranged it is preferable to provide a hot dinner for
them.*

In large households a hot dinner for the servants is
a matter of course, but in small households, where
there is a great deal of cooking to do for the family, the
cook not unfrequently gives the servants a cold dinner
to save trouble; but considerate mistresses arrange

with the cook what they wish the servants to have, and the dinner is submitted on a slate for their approval, according to the contents of the larder, in the same manner that the family dinner is submitted to them, and a mistress makes any alterations or suggestions she may think proper.

With regard to beer, the usual allowance per day is - for men-servants - for lunch a pint, for dinner a pint, and for supper a pint; and for the women-servants - for lunch half-a-pint, for dinner a pint, and for supper half-a-pint. It is a very general rule in households to allow the servants beer-money instead of beer, from motives of economy, it is considered that it causes less waste, and that it is less indiscriminately given away, and that there is less incentive to idlers to hang about the house in expectation of a pint of beer. In town this is sensible plan to follow, but in the country, where beer is home-brewed by the butler, it is seldom followed, and is inhospitable and over close, as all who come to the house necessarily come from some distance; besides, the cost of the home-brewed small-beer thus consumed is but trifling.

But this plan of allowing servants beer-money in the place of beer has disadvantages, if it has advantages. If men-servants are not especially well-principled, sober, and steady, they not unfrequently spend their beer-money in spirits in the nearest public-house, or they idle away their time by constantly going out to get "a pint of beer."

Women-servants, on the contrary, when allowed beer-money, invariably dispense with beer altogether.

Beer or beer-money is now seldom allowed to young women-servants. Total abstainers maintain that beer is unnecessary, and that to drink it is more a habit than a need.

Some few mistresses, from motives of strict economy, put their servants on board wages, even when the family is at home.

For men-servants 12s. to 16s. is the usual allowance, and for women-servants 10s. to 14s. per week.

When this arrangement is made, the meals take place at the same hours as when ordered by the mistress of the house. Such an arrangement does not as a rule work well, and therefore it is seldom followed.

The servants in these cases club together, and the cook caters for them; but if there is a saving in this plan, and there certainly is when the family live principally upon game, and poultry, and entrées, rather than upon joints of beef and mutton, it is not one that is very popular with either mistresses or servants: it renders servants in a way independent of their masters and mistresses; they lose the feeling of being members of one household and dependent upon the kindness and consideration of its master and mistress, whereas this bond should be strengthened rather than weakened if faithful service is wished for and expected.

The usual hour for tea in large and small establishments, is from four to five; the upper servants have tea in either the steward's room or the housekeeper's room, and the tea-table is laid respectively by either the steward's-room boy or the still-room maid; in the servants' hall the tea-table is laid by the servants'-hall boy, and in the kitchen it is laid by the cook. The tea-tray containing the cups and saucers, teapot, &c., is placed at the top of the table, on the tablecover, a white table-cloth not being used for tea in either of these apartments; a small knife and plate are placed for each person, and bread, butter, dry toast, and plum-cake are placed on the table. The housekeeper pours out the tea in the steward's room and in the housekeeper's room, the upper housemaid or head kitchen-maid makes tea for the under servants' hall, in the kitchen the cook pours out the tea.

In many houses each servant has an allowance of tea and sugar, which is given out once a week or once a month, the average being one pound of tea per month and two pounds of loaf sugar per month; in other houses an allowance of tea and sugar is not made, but the quantity used is regulated by the housekeeper or cook, who keeps it within these limits.

The usual hour for supper is half-past eight or nine. In large establishments hot suppers are allowed in the steward's room and housekeeper's room; and the entrées and sweets that have been served in the dining-room are generally sent into the housekeeper's room for supper, while other mistresses only allow the joints to be eaten, and require the entrées and sweets to be kept to form part of their own luncheon on the following day. The supper-table is laid by the steward's-room boy or still-room maid, two knives and forks, a dessert spoon, a tumbler and wine-glass, are placed for each person.

In a few large establishments wine is allowed in the housekeeper's room and steward's room, averaging three or four bottles per week. The housekeeper, groom of the chambers, butler, or house-steward helps or carves at supper. The still-room maid waits at table in the housekeeper's room, and the steward's-room boy waits in the steward's room; but it is only in the house of the very wealthy where a house-steward is kept, and where there is consequently a steward's room and steward's-room boy.

It is far more usual for the upper servants to have their meals in the housekeeper's room. The servant's-hall supper consists of cold meat, hot vegetables, and bread and cheese; the table is laid by the servant's-hall boy, or by the scullery-maid; two knives, a fork, and a tumbler are placed for each person; the under butler or head footman and head housemaid carve, or help at table. In the kitchen the supper-table is laid by the cook, who also carves. In these small establishments cold meat and bread and cheese are allowed for supper; and in some very economical families meat for supper is not given, and only bread and cheese is provided; and it is an understood thing that what is left from the dining-room dinner is not to be eaten in the kitchen, but to be kept for breakfast and luncheon.

A bell is rung for breakfast, dinner, and supper, but it is not rung for tea. Half an hour is allowed for breakfast, the same for tea and supper; an hour for dinner.

Considerate masters and mistresses endeavour, as far as possible, not to ring for their servants during the hours allotted for meals.

OPENING THE DOOR, AND ANNOUNCING VISITORS

Opening the door to visitors and announcing visitors are light yet important duties in the every-day routine of a servant's work.

In a large establishment where a staff of man-servants are kept these duties are performed necessarily in the most efficient and orthodox manner.

In smaller establishments, where the footman has perhaps been recently promoted to the post of butler, and a new footman has also been engaged whose character with regard to honesty and sobriety is satisfactory, but whose capabilities have yet to be discovered, or when both butler and footman are new to their respective positions, and are more or less untried servants, or when a single-handed man-servant is new to his work, or a parlour-maid is new to hers, then it is that these duties, simple though they are, put the servant's training to the test, and the mistress to the blush.

There is no surer indication of the manner in which a household is conducted than is conveyed in this "*answering the door.*"

To keep a visitor standing on the doorstep of a house for five minutes or more argues that the attendance in that house is very lax, and that the mistress of it is to blame, and prepares one for the slovenly, untidy, half-sleepy appearance the servant will probably present when at last he opens the door, or for the bare arms, black face, and dirty apron of the female servant when she ventures to appear.

One would imagine that the custom amongst overworked maids of going out into the front area to obtain a view of the applicant for admission, on the chance of being able to hold communication with them from below, and to discover their business without the trouble of answering the door, was confined to that much-enduring class, were if not the footman in gentlemen's families residing in the heart of fashionable London are given to this impertinent mode of proceeding, perhaps excusable in a maid of all work, but inexcusable on the part of a footman. A woman left in charge of a house who puts her head out of the window or looks up the area is justified in thus reconnoitring before answering the door; she is on the defensive, and an ugly customer or suspicious looking person she would be wise to parley with from her vantage point above or below, namely, the window or the area. Such tactics on the part of a lone, lorn woman are to be recommended and commended.

When a footman has not been informed whether his mistress is at home to visitors or not, he either leaves them at the door, or ushers them into the drawing-room, on the change of her being at home to them, and if not inclined or able to receive visitors, some little awkwardness is occasioned both in giving and receiving such message; the servant looks foolish, and the visitor looks and feels annoyed that the answer of "Not at home" was not at once given.

"Not at home" is the received formula in society to express a lady's inability or disinclination to receive visitors; some persons not understanding it in this light, take it to mean a direct untruth, and will not allow their servants to make use of it, but it is in reality the recognised mode of insuring privacy without entering into explanations as to the why and the wherefore. For instance, if a mistress of a house were but slightly indisposed or overtired, and she were to be denied to visitors on the plea of not being well enough to see them, she would doubtless have callers the next day to inquire after her health.

Too much engaged to see visitors is also not a polite answer to give to a caller, but when a lady occupied with domestic matters, going into her household accounts, examining the wardrobes of her children, or giving directions about her own, a servant has no alternative but to say that his mistress is engaged, if the formula of "not at home" is objected to. In all cases when the answer of "not at home" is returned, whether the mistress of the house is really out, or simply "not at home" to visitors, a well-mannered servant enters into no particulars as to when she went out, where she has gone, and when she may be expected to return, but restricts himself to this formula, and receives the cards left, or the message, if any, the one in silence, and the other with "yes, ma'am."

The mistress of a house usually informs the butler whether she intends being at home to visitors both in the morning and in the afternoon. "If any one calls this morning, Smith, I am not at home"; or if she wished to see visitors she would probably say "I am at home to any one who calls." But ladies who make a practice of being at home to all callers, allow it to be understood that they are at home to every one, unless an order is given to the contrary. When a mistress of a house is not down herself to give the order, she sends it through her maid. The butler is expected to inform the footman of his mistress's intention.

In grand establishments where a groom of the chambers, a butler, and three or four footmen are kept, one of the footmen opens the door, the other three stand in the hall, and the groom of the chambers proceeds the visitors to the drawing-room, and announces them to his mistress.

In this class of establishment the footmen wear full-dress livery, knee breeches, silk stockings, and powdered hair.

When an establishment consists of a butler and two footmen, it is the butler's duty to answer the door in the morning, while the footmen are engaged in pantry work, which, in some houses, is very heavy at this time of the day.

Where a butler and one footman are kept it is again the butler's duty to answer the door in the morning, while the footman is engaged in pantry work.

Where a single-handed man-servant is kept, the lady's-maid not unfrequently undertakes to answer the door in the morning to admit of the man-servant getting through his work before luncheon. Where a page only is kept the same plan is generally followed.

Where a parlour-maid is kept, the same arrangement is made, that of the lady's-maid answering the door in the morning that the parlour-maid may also get through her pantry and other work. Where no lady's-maid is kept, then the mistress of a house arranges, when engaging her servants, that the cook is to answer the door from ten to twelve, to enable the parlour-maid to get through the heaviest part of her work.

This plan is equally followed in those small households where no lady's-maid is kept, and where the house-maid is engaged to be parlour-maid as well as house-maid. If a mistress of a house, when engaging her servants, is not careful in attending to this point, she will find that a servant cannot perform his or her work in a satisfactory manner if constantly called away from it when in the midst of it; neither can they present a creditable appearance, if compelled to hasten from the pantry to the front hall. Servants, if allowed to arrange this matter between themselves, would probably oblige each other to-day, and refuse assistance to-morrow.

Some ladies have an objection to the door being answered by a maid-servant, when they keep a man-servant, and expect him to get through his work by eleven or half-past, but it is only in small households where this arrangement can be carried out.

In ordinary sized households twelve o'clock is the usual hour when a single-handed man-servant or parlour-maid may be expected to resume this duty. Before that hour people principally call at a house on business; they call to take orders and measurements, they bring articles that have been ordered, they bring things on approbation, or the collector calls for accounts, great and small, for King's taxes and Parish rates, water and gas rates.

Orders that belong to the kitchen department, the baker, the butcher, the fishmonger, the greengrocer, &c.; are necessarily answered by the cook at the area-door, or back-door; but those calling for orders at the front door of a house, generally have business direct with the master or mistress of it.

Parcels and small packages are not left at the area-door, but are taken to the front door. Only things appertaining to the kitchen are taken there.

In the afternoon, from three to six, where a groom of the chambers, a butler, and three or four footmen are kept, the one who is termed the ladies footman is the one who "goes out with the carriage," as only on the occasion of a drawing-room or a state entertainment are two footmen in attendance with the carriage; either of the other footmen opens the door; but the groom of the chambers and the butler remain in the hall during the hours for calling.

Where a butler and two footmen are kept, one footman - the ladies' footman - goes out with the carriage, and the second footman and the butler answer the door; where only one footman is kept, it is the butler's duty to answer the door when the footman is out with the carriage.

Where a single-handed man-servant is kept, he goes out with the carriage, and the lady's-maid or house-maid answers the door accordingly as the mistress of the house has arranged; the same arrangement is made where a page is kept, his duty of answering the door - when he is out with the carriage - is performed by the lady's-maid or house-maid. When one man-servant or page is kept, if sent on messages by their mistresses, the same arrangement holds good, but considerate mistresses avoid as far as possible interrupting their one man-servant or page at his morning work.

In answering the door to visitors, on the bell being rung, the footman opens the hall-door wide; he does not hold the handle, or the door itself, in his hand, but opens it to its fullest extent, and stands in the centre of the doorway. If the visitor is driving, her footman should inquire of him if his mistress is at home, and should say, "Is Mrs. A. at home?" He should not say, "Lady B. is come to see Mrs. A.," or make any communications of a like confidential character; if a visitor has not a footman with her, and many ladies who patronize hired broughams and victorias are often obliged to drive out unattended by a man-servant, the footman opening the door should go at once to the carriage, and the lady should ask if Mrs. A. is at home.

Ladies driving without a man-servant to act as footman, either desire the coachman to leave his box and ring the bell and mount to it again as quickly as may be, or the coachman hails a passing boy and politely asks him to ring that bell, indicating with his whip the bell in question; he makes the request with a certain amount of persuasion in his voice; street boys are, as he well knows, very independent, and much given to "chaff"; and were one to follow the course of a driver of a hired brougham, one might observe that boys with baskets are always selected for the office of bell-ringer in preference to boys without baskets, and would hear him say, " *Will you oblige me by ringing that bell?*" or, "*Jist you ring that bell, there's a good lad! Pull it hard, please.*" Ladies with more sense and less dignity, when they cannot afford to keep a man-servant, get out of the carriage and ring the door-bell for themselves, preferring this independence of action to street boys being pressed into their service.

Whether the visitor is driving attended or unattended by a footman, if the lady of the house is not at home, cards are given to the servant answering the door. If she is at home, the servant of the lady calling opens the carriage-door for her, or if she has no servant with her, the one answering the door performs this office.

When the footman has informed the servant, or the visitor herself, that his mistress is at home, the butler, who is standing in the hall, comes forward to usher her to the drawing-room, and walks before her a few steps in advance either upstairs to the drawing-room door, or across the hall, or down the corridor, if the drawing-room is on the ground-floor.

At the door of the drawing-room the servant asks, "What name, if you please, ma'am?" and upon the name being told him, he opens the drawing-room door wide, and announces Mrs. A. If his mistress is sitting in the back drawing-room or boudoir, and is not near enough to hear the announcement, he goes forward and repeats the name of the visitor to her, leaving the visitor to seat herself in the front drawing-room. If, on the contrary, the mistress of a house generally sits in the back drawing-room, the servant, being aware of this, announces visitors at the door of that room; if the mistress of a house is not in the drawing-room, the servant does not announce the name of the visitor, but ushers her into the drawing-room, and informs her that he will let his mistress know that she is there.

Where a groom of chambers is kept, it is his duty to announce visitors instead of the butler; and where there is only a single-handed man-servant, page or parlour-maid kept, it is their duty to answer the door and announce the visitors in the manner above described. If the visitor is walking she or he is received in a similar manner by the servants of a house.

Were a gentlemen and lady to arrive at a house simultaneously, the lady would be announced before the gentlemen; the servant must not be permitted to couple the names of visitors and announce them as Mr. Brown and Mrs. Smith. When he is announcing a husband and wife, he says, Mr. and Mrs. Brown, or a brother and sister, Mr. and Mrs. Smith; or a mother and daughter, Mrs. and Miss Jones. If two ladies not bearing the same name pay a call together, their names are coupled thus - Mrs. Smith and Miss. Brown. If two ladies arrive simultaneously, their names are not coupled the servant says, announcing them at the same moment, Mrs. Smith, Mrs. Brown. Neither would the names of two gentlemen be coupled, unless they arrived in company, but they would be announced at the same moment thus - Captain Jones, Captain Smith.

It would be in extremely bad taste were a servant to leave one visitor waiting in the hall while he announced the other. Were the door-bell to ring when a single-handed man-servant, page or parlour-maid as about to usher a visitor to the drawing-room, they must in no case leave the visitor on or at the foot of the stairs while returning to open the door.

Announcing Visitors.

In announcing persons of rank, the full title is used of marquis and marchioness, earl and countess, viscount and viscountess, baron and baroness, but the Lord and Lady are substituted in the case of an English baron and his wife. In announcing a duke or duchess, the words His or Her Grace are not used, and a servant should say, The Duke and Duchess on Monmouth. The sons and daughters or dukes and marquises are announced by their titles - christian and surname.

The daughters of earls are also announced as Lady Mary Blank, but the youngest sons of earls and the sons and daughters of earls and the sons and daughters of viscounts and barons are not announced by the title of Honourable, as it is a courtesy title never used in announcing visitors. The Honourable Mr., Mrs, or Miss. Blank are announced as Mr., Mrs., or Miss Blank.

Baronets are announced as Sir George or Sir John Blank, but the word Bart. is, it is needless to say, not used when announcing baronets.

It is a vulgar error to style the wives of baronets Lady John or Lady George, according to the christian names of their husbands; they are announced as they are addressed, Lady Blank or Lady Dash. It would be equally vulgar to announce the wife of an admiral, general, colonel, major, or captain, as Mrs General

Smith, or Mrs. Captain Brown, &c.

With regard to showing visitors out, as soon as the drawing-room bell is rung the servants or servant should be in readiness in the hall to show the visitor out. If the visitor is driving, a footman or man-servant beckons to the coachman to drive up, and when he sees her descending the stairs he calls out "Coming out" as a signal that her footman is to open the carriage door. In the country when the drawing-room bell is rung before the departure of a visitor, it is answered by the butler, and the order is given for the visitor's carriage to be brought round.  The butler gives this order to the footman, who transmits it to the coachman, who is probably being regaled with beer in the servants' hall while his mistress is refreshing herself with tea in the drawing-room. When the horses are put-to and the carriage is in readiness, the butler announces the fact to the visitor, and says "Your carriage is up, please ma'am," or "Your ladyship's carriage is up."

The mode of announcing guests at all entertainments is similar to that already described. Dinner guests are conducted to the cloak-room by the foot-man who opens the door to them. The butler or groom of the chambers awaits them at the foot of the staircase or in the corridor, and ushers them to the drawing-room, asking them their names at the door. When a cloak-room is not provided for gentlemen as well as ladies, extra accommodation is provided in the hall, or corridor.

At Dances, Balls, Private Theatricals, At Homes, and large Five o'clock Teas, guests are first ushered to the cloak-room, and are then asked by the butler, who waits in the hall for the purpose, if they will first go to the tea-room; the formula in use for these occasions is, "Will you take tea, ma'am?" If the guests desire refreshments in the shape of tea, coffee, &c., they are shown to the tea-room, and on leaving the tea-room they are ushered to the drawing-room or ball-room, and duly announced in the manner before described.

When calls are made for business purposes, the footman or man-servant who answers the door does not leave the person who calls to see his master or mistress standing on the doorstep while he ascertains if his master or mistress will see them, but asks them to take a seat in the hall. If a servant were in doubt, as he not unfrequently is, as to whether the call is a business or friendly one, it would be correct for him to say, "I beg your pardon, ma'am, but do you wish to see my mistress on business?" And if the answer were in the affirmative, he would then say, "I will take up your card, if you please." In which case, he would take the card to his mistress on a salver, or he would send it to her by her maid if she were not in the drawing-room. If he took the card to her himself, he would say, "A person has called to see you, please, ma'am, and is waiting in the hall;" or he would say, "A lady wishes to know if you will see her for five minutes, and has sent up her card, if you please, ma'am."

It is necessary that servants in town should exercise a certain amount of discretion as to whom they admit into the presence of their master of mistress. Persons having legitimate business at a house generally evince no reluctance at stating the nature of it to the servant in attendance, while those persons who are shy at making it known are persons to be guarded against.

Well-trained servants do not gossip at the hall-door with every idle messenger inclined to do so, but after giving whatever answer they may be, do not further detain them.

THE DUTIES OF
A HOUSE-STEWARD
A GROOM OF THE CHAMBERS
A VALET

THE HOUSE STEWARD. A house-steward is only considered necessary in households which are conducted on a very extensive scale, and where the outlay of money and the general expenses render housekeeping accounts of sufficient importance to demand the attention of a competent person.

Sometimes the house-steward also undertakes the office of land-steward, in which case his duties take a wider range. The house-steward has a sitting room for his use in the mansion, but the land steward has a house allotted to him, and is a very different class of individual to the house-steward, who is, strictly, a sort of head butler, exempt from menial duties. His duty is to engage the men and women-servants, with the exception of the family, ladies' maids, nurses, and valet; to pay them their wages, and to dismiss them. To order everything that is necessary for the wants of the household; to pay the household bills; to keep the household books; and to see that order and regularity is maintained amongst the servants.

The house-steward is responsible to his master for the money that passes through his hands, and usually submits the household books for his approval once a month.

The house-steward is not a livery-servant, and does not receive an allowance for his clothes.

THE GROOM OF THE CHAMBERS, like the house-steward, is a class of servant belonging to the households of the very wealthy. He is also a species of butler; but one from whom menial work is expected.

His principal duty is to announce visitors to his mistress; and he may be looked upon as the custodian of the sitting-rooms, besides being on duty in the corridors, in case his services should be required to show any strange guests to their rooms, or to open or close doors. He remains in the front hall in the afternoon, in readiness to announce visitors, or to receive the cards left. He makes the round of the sitting-rooms three or four times during the day, to ascertain the everything is in order. He assists in waiting at breakfast, luncheon, and dinner. He stands outside the drawing-room or library door, to open it for the guests as they severally come down before dinner. He assists in carrying in the tea and coffee into the drawing-room after dinner, and is in attendance in the hall when the family retire for the night, to light the bedroom candles.

It is customary for noblemen and very wealthy gentry to be waited upon by this description of upper servant.

A groom of the chambers does not wear livery, but receives an allowance for plain clothes in addition to his wages.

VALETS are generally kept by single gentlemen and by elderly gentlemen, and seldom by married men, unless by noblemen or persons of considerable wealth. Single men require the services of a valet, unless they keep a butler and footman, when the butler acts as valet. Elderly gentlemen often require the services of a valet in addition to those of the men-servants of their establishments, as constant personal attendance cannot satisfactorily be given by a butler who has other duties to perform.

Young men who pay rounds of visits to country houses cannot easily dispense with a valet. Sportsmen, and men given to hunting and shooting, find the services of one invaluable.

Amongst the duties of a valet are the following:- to

brush his master's clothes, to clean his top-boots, shooting, walking, and dress-boots; to carry up the water for his master's bath, to put out his things for dressing; to shave him, if necessary; to assist him in dressing; to pack and unpack his clothes when travelling; to put out his master's things for dinner; to carry up the hot water to his dressing-room.

To load for him when out shooting; to stand behind his master's chair at dinner; and more especially to wait upon his master and the lady taken down to dinner by him. When at home he is expected to wait at his master's breakfast, and at the family luncheon and dinner; he attends to his master's wardrobe, and sees that everything is in repair and in order. A valet to an elderly gentlemen, besides performing these duties, renders any services that the state of his master's health may require; such as sitting up at night, carrying him up and down stairs during the day, when required to do so, or sleep in his room at night.

Where a courier is engaged to travel with a gentlemen, his duty is also to valet him.

A valet is not a livery-servant; he does not receive an allowance for clothes, and his master's left-off clothes are given to him.

THE BUTLER'S DUTIES

The office of butler is as ancient as it is responsible, and in all establishments, from the largest to the smallest, he is the head of his department, and is answerable for the property placed under his charge, and for the proper performance of the duties of those under him, viz., the footman or footmen.

The butler is supposed to have served his apprenticeship in domestic service, first as under-footman, then as head footman or under-butler; he is, therefore, able to judge of the amount of work that a footman is equal to getting through, and how it should be done.

Some masters and mistresses object to engaging a married man as butler.

They consider that a married man is likely to

spend too much of his time at home, and to be consequently away from his master's house when most wanted; and, further, that the cares and expenses of a family probably militate against his being as well dressed and as smart-looking a servant as an unmarried man would presumably be.

They also fear that, having a wife and family to support, great temptation is placed in his way, temptation which some masters consider their servants should not be exposed to, in case of their being too weak to resist it.

Great poverty might induce a father or husband to commit acts of dishonesty, and to become unfaithful to trust reposed in him, which a single man would not be tempted to commit; as, for instance, if the family of a butler were in great distress through the illness of his wife and children, or through other causes, having the charge of the family plate he might be tempted to raise money at a pawnbroker's upon any portion or article that was not in general use, or likely to be required before he was able to redeem it. This is by no means an imaginary temptation, but is one of frequent occurrence, as the police reports testify.

Again, the wine under a butler's charge is a temptation to a married man whose wife is ailing and very much in need of strengthening things.

Half bottles of wine and whole bottles of wine are

under such circumstances not unlikely to find their way to the butler's home; while he justifies himself for this lapse of trust by the specious reasoning that a bottle or two of wine can make no possible difference to a master whose cellars are so bountifully stocked, while to his wife it makes all the difference in the matter of regaining health and strength!

This is but the weak side of human nature, and there are married butlers worthy of the trust reposed in them, perhaps because they are not so greatly tried as are others. Still, the generality of masters and mistresses disapprove of their butlers being married men for the before-mentioned reasons, while others, again, consider that a butler who is married is likely to be more steady in the household than one who is unmarried; and single ladies or widow ladies attach great importance to the fact of their butler being a married man, and rely upon his good character as a sufficient guarantee of his honesty.

If the butler takes a situation, representing himself as an unmarried man when he is in reality a married man, he is liable to be dismissed without notice.

Insobriety is a very common failing amongst butlers, and one that cannot be too greatly guarded against on the part of masters and mistresses when making inquiries respecting the character of a butler.

A butler in a large establishment, where perhaps

three footmen are kept, has not as much actual pantry work to do as would devolve upon him in a household where only one footman is kept, but his duties are quite arduous, although they take another direction.

The establishment being on a large scale, increases his responsibility, and the amount of company kept greatly increases the work of the pantry.

The plate chest is in the charge of the butler, and an inventory of its contents is given on its being made over to him, and he is responsible to his master for its safety. If any article is lost, or missing, or damaged while in his charge, his master holds him answerable for it, therefore it behoves a butler to be extremely careful as to whom he admits into his pantry when the plate is being cleaned, and also to exercise great caution when engaging extra help to assist at dinner parties and balls!

It is the butler's duty, every night before retiring to rest, to see that the plate in everyday use is carefully put away, and also to give it out in the morning to be cleaned. He also gives out plate used at dinner parties or balls, and see that it is properly cleaned for use.

His next responsibility is the wine cellar. The cellar book is the check upon the butler as to the quantity of wine drunk in a given time. The master of every establishment keeps the keys of his wine cellars, and gives out so many dozens of wine for the consumption of the household, either once a week, or once a month. The butler's duty is to enter into the cellar book the amount of wine given out, and the number of bottles drunk per day, whether claret, champagne, sherry, or port.

On the occasion of a dinner party or a dance, a master of a house gives out so many dozens of wine, according to the number of guests invited to dinner or dance. The wine thus given into a butler's charge is kept by him in a separate cellar, of which he keeps the key.

It is the butler's duty to decant the wine for daily use, both for luncheon and dinner, and to put away decanters of wine after each meal. Bottling wine and brewing beer are two important duties performed by a butler in both large and small establishments, although brewing beer is exclusively confined to households in the country. A master of a house tastes, chooses, and buys his own wine, and does not depute his butler to do this for him.

Wine sent in for bottling undergoes the proper process of fining before it is delivered, and a butler should not venture upon introducing any mixtures of his own concoction for the purpose of fining it, but should bottle it as soon as it is in a proper condition for the purpose, it having remained sufficiently long in the cellar to become clear. In bottling valuable wine he should not only rely upon his judgement as to the condition of the wine, but should, if not thoroughly experienced in the matter, submit a sample to his master for his approval.

A butler should have his bottles in readiness several days beforehand, and when engaged in bottling wine, he probably rises as early as four or five in the morning that his cellar work may not materially interfere with his duties of the day.

In bottling sherry, the wine that is drawn off after the cask has been tilted, is kept by the butler in his cellar for the use of the cook, and given out as required.

Country butlers greatly pride themselves upon the excellent beer they brew, but those who have to drink it are apt to consider it rather hard and a trifle sour; but as it is brewed for consumption of the household, and seldom makes its appearance in the dining-room, those who are obliged to drink it, if they have an opinion as to its demerits, are not in a position to express it. The butler usually selects a week in which to brew, when his master and mistress are away from home, that he may have sufficient time to devote to the occupation. But bottling wine and brewing beer are occasional rather than every day duties, and the every day duties of a butler consist of the following.

Where a valet is not kept, it is a butler's duty to valet his master and when acting in the capacity of a valet, he receives the left-off wardrobe of his master, which makes his situation a more lucrative one.

When two or three footmen are kept, a butler waits at breakfast, luncheon, tea, and dinner, and overlooks the arrangements of the table for each meal.

During the afternoon it is a butler's duty to remain in the front hall in readiness to announce visitors.

It is the butler's duty throughout the day to see that everything is in its place and in order, in readiness for use in the drawing-room, morning-room, and library; the blinds up or down as the case may be, writing tables in due order, books rearranged, newspapers cut, aired, and folded for use, fires attended to by the footman, &c., &c.

In households where one footman is kept, a large portion of the pantry work falls to the share of the butler: he lays the breakfast table, waits at breakfast, and clears away the breakfast things; he assists in cleaning the plate and in attending to the lamps; he waits at luncheon; and when the footman has to go out with the carriage early in the afternoon, a butler clears away the luncheon and lays the dinner-table.

While the footman is out with the carriage, the butler answers the door, attends to the fires in dining-room, drawing-rooms, and various sitting-rooms of the house, and in the autumn, winter and early spring, he closes the shutters in the sitting-rooms before the footman's return, and prepares the five-o'clock tea in readiness for the return of his mistress.

A butler is usually allowed to go out in the morning from twelve to one, and again from half-past nine to eleven, in town establishments.

FOOTMEN'S DUTIES

In households where two or three footmen are kept, heads of families make a point of keeping tall footmen, and having men of equal height to avoid the incongruity of appearance that men-servants of unequal height would present. Where only one footman is kept, his height is immaterial, and smartness and neatness of appearance are alone required of him.

As we have mentioned already, two footmen are not unfrequently kept in lieu of a butler and one footman; and when this is the case, although the pantry work is equally divided, yet the head footman as he is termed, receives higher wages than the second footman, and has the charge of the plate and of the wine given out.

Where two or three footmen and a butler are kept the head footman, although in livery, is termed the under butler. He does not go out with the carriage; it is the duty of the second footman to do so; it is the under butler's duty to remain in the front hall to answer the door to visitors during the afternoon. Where a butler and one footman are kept, it is the one footman's duty to go out with the carriage.

What is termed the lady's footman is usually the second footman where three are kept. In the division of work, where two or three footmen are kept, the third footman performs such duties as bringing in coals and wood, cleaning knives and boots, &c., and in the country pumping or drawing the water for daily use; while the under butler and second footman clean the plate, trim and clean the lamps, and where a still-room maid is not kept, they also wash the breakfast and tea services in use.

The daily round of duties are as follows:- To rise at half-past six in summer and seven in winter; to take coals to the sitting-room; to clean the boots; to trim the lamps; clean the plate; to lay the breakfast-table for the family; to carry in the breakfast; to wait at breakfast; to remove the breakfast things; to answer the door in the morning after twelve o'clock, to take out notes if required; to lay the luncheon-table; to take in the luncheon; to wait at table; to clear the table;

to wash the silver and glass used at luncheon; to lay the dinner-table; to go out with the carriage in the afternoon; to answer the door to visitors; to close the shutters in the sitting-rooms; to attend to the fires therein throughout the day and evening; to prepare and assist in carrying in the afternoon tea; to clear the table after tea; to wash and put away the china; to wait at dinner; to clear the dinner-table; to assist in putting away the plate; to wash the glass and silver used at dinner and dessert; to prepare and assist in carrying in the coffee to the dining room, and coffee also into the drawing-room; to be in attendance in the front hall when dinner guests are leaving the house, on the occasion of a dinner-party; to attend to requirements of the gentlemen in the smoking-room; to attend to the lighting of the house, generally, as soon as it is dusk, whether lighted with gas, lamps, or candles; to clean, arrange, and have in readiness the flat silver candlesticks, before the dressing-room bell rings in winter, and by ten o'clock in summer; to go out with the carriage when it is ordered in the evening; to valet the young gentlemen of the family.

When only one footman is kept, the butler assists him in various of these duties; but in every case the footman goes out with the carriage, afternoon and evening.

Footmen are usually allowed two suits of livery a

year. Some heads of families give higher wages and allow their servants to find their own liveries; but this latter plan does not work so satisfactorily as the former, and footmen who find their own liveries are not, as a rule, so well dressed as those whose liveries are found for them.

Where two or three footmen are kept, the under butler and the second footman are expected to wait at breakfast. Where two footmen are kept, the under butler only assists the butler in waiting at breakfast; but where one footman is kept, he does not do so by reason of his having so much work to get through.

A mooted point in some households is whether a footman is expected to carry up coals for bedroom fires. The general rule is that it is the footman's duty to carry coals to dinning-room, library, drawing-rooms, &c., and also to the best bedrooms.

THE DUTIES OF
A SINGLE-HANDED MAN-SERVANT
A PAGE-BOY

THE SINGLE-HANDED MAN-SERVANT performs the combined duties of butler and footman. The class who keep this order of servant is a large one, as it comprises those possessing very moderate incomes, and very small incomes. There are, of course, exceptions to this rule, viz., those who possess fairly good incomes, yet keep but little company, and live what is termed very quietly, who can afford, were they so inclined, to keep two men-servants, but prefer to keep one man-servant only, in or out of livery.

A single-handed man-servant is not a liveried servant, although he is allowed two suits of clothes a year, or extra wages to find his own clothes. A single-handed man-servant is expected to be an experienced servant, and to have lived as footman under a good butler; but a trustworthy and well-trained servant of this class is not always easy to meet with. The wages of a single-handed man-servant are not as high as are those of a butler; while the place is a far harder one, and requires no little method, industry, and briskness to perform the many duties required of him in a satisfactory manner.

His duties include the following: to rise early, so that before his breakfast he may have completed the rougher work of the day, such as getting in coals and wood, cleaning the knives and boots, etc.; his duty is to valet the gentlemen of the family; to brush their clothes, to carry them up and put them out for dressing, to carry up water for the gentlemen's baths, shaving-water, etc.; to lay the breakfast for the family; to be dressed to carrying the breakfast, although not expected to wait at that meal; to take away the breakfast things, to wash and replace in the pantry cupboard; to trim and clean the lamps; to clean the plate; to lay the luncheon, to wait at luncheon when required to do so, to clear away the luncheon, and wash the glass and silver used; to attend to the sitting-room fires; to be in readiness to answer the drawing-room bell; to answer the door in the afternoon, when not out with the carriage; to go out with the carriage afternoon and evening when required; to close the shutters in the sitting-rooms; to keep the front hall in order; to put coats, hats and umbrellas in their places; to prepare and carry in the afternoon tea, to clear it away, wash and replace the china, &c., to lay the table for dinner, to wait at dinner, to clear the table, to wash the glass and silver and put everything in its place; to carry the coffee into the drawing -room, to clear it away, wash and replace the china, etc.; to prepare the candles for the sitting-rooms, and to have the flat candlesticks in readiness in the hall; to see that the doors and windows of the house are properly secured; to draw the beer for the servants' lunch, dinner, and supper.

The single-handed man-servant is not entrusted with the cellar-book, and very little wine, if any, is placed in his charge, the master or mistress preferring to take charge of it themselves; he is not expected to bottle wine or to brew beer; but he is often expected to make himself useful in the house when required; to move and clean furniture; to clean windows, mirrors, chandeliers, etc.

IN SOME FEW HOUSEHOLDS A PAGE is kept instead of a man-servant; but it is not a general practice to do so, and people who cannot afford to keep a man-servant, find that a parlour-maid is more useful and efficient than is a page and far less pretentious in appearance. In hotels and clubs a page is found useful to carry messages, notes, etc.; but in private families a page-boy is anything but a satisfactory servant.

He generally enters into service at an age when boys are most troublesome and require keeping in order.

If there are children in the family the page plays with them, instead of attending to his work; he is not strong enough or big enough to lift and carry large trays up and downstairs.

A page is only at his best in those families where a butler and footman are kept, as in large households a page is occasionally kept in addition to the men-servants, and where the work is comparatively heavy, when he assists the footman in many of his duties; but the single-handed page is rather an obsolete servant, and is principally to be found in those families where conform is sacrificed to would-be gentility. When a page is kept in these small families his duties are those of a single-handed man-servant, with the exception of drawing the beer for the servants, and seeing that the house is closed at night.

A page is allowed two suits of livery a year and one working suit, and this livery is the property of the master and mistress, and a page is not entitled to claim it when leaving his situation.

THE DUTIES OF
THE COACHMAN AND GROOMS

The duties of a coachman vary according to the position he occupies; whether he is head coachman, second coachman with grooms under him, or whether he is coachman with one or two grooms under him, or coachman and groom in one.

Where two coachmen are kept, the stable department is on a large scale and two carriages are often ordered at the same hour, when the head coachman drives a pair of horses and the second coachman drives one horse. The head coachman invariably drives a pair of horses in the barouche or other open carriage, and the second coachman the one-horse brougham.

The night work, such as driving the family to a ball, or driving to and from the railway-station, is the duty of the second coachman.

It is the duty of the head coachman to see that those under him perform their work in a thoroughly efficient manner, and that the horses are properly fed and groomed, the carriages and harness are thoroughly cleaned, the stables and harness-room are in perfect order. Occasionally the second coachman's duty is to exercise the horses, and to assist in cleaning the carriages and harness in use.

A head coachman's is an office of considerable trust. Whether he orders the hay, corn, straw, &c., or whether it is ordered by his master, he has the charge of it, and the expenses of the stables in other directions, which are considerable, are also under his management.

Where two coachmen and as many grooms are kept the carriage is probably out three times a day; where one coachman and groom are dept, it is usual to have a carriage out twice only, a pair of horses in the afternoon, and a pair, or single horse in the evening, or a pair in the morning and again in the afternoon. A horse for night work is frequently kept when the carriage is much required in the evening, and when the condition of the carriage horse is considered.

The coachman's duty is to assist the groom in cleaning the carriages and the harness, and in grooming the horses. Where one coachman is kept without a groom under him, he only expects to go out once a day, either morning, afternoon, or evening, that is, if a pair of horses are kept and two carriages, and they are expect to look up to the mark; but if the coachman has only the charge of one horse and one carriage, brougham, waggonette, or victoria, the carriage can be had out twice a day without overworking the coachman.

In some families coachmen have their meals in the house with the other servants, in others they have board wages allowed them, and rooms over the stables or a cottage rent free. A coachman submits his book of incidental expenses of the stables to his master either weekly, fortnightly, or monthly.

A groom's principal duty is to attend to the horses and to exercise them; and to groom them throughout the day after they have been out, to clean the carriages and harness, feed the horses, &c. The stables are expected to be ready for his masters inspection by nine or ten o'clock each morning.

A pad-groom is in attendance upon his master and mistress out riding, whether to convert or elsewhere, and has the charge of the saddle horses.

THE HOUSEKEEPER'S DUTIES

The duties of a housekeeper are, in the majority of establishments, united to those of a cook or lady's-maid, but in large establishments the office of house-keeper is a distinct one.

In households where the domestics number from five-and-twenty to thirty, the office of housekeeper is no sinecure, more especially in the country, when the heads of establishments entertain largely, and when the house is, during the winter months, more or less full of guests:- country house parties include not only guests but probably a large number of servants, who have to be accommodated and catered for.

In this class of establishment the sole management of the female servants rests with the housekeeper; it is her duty to engage and to dismiss them, with the exception of the nurse, lady's-maid, and cook, whom the mistress of the house herself engages.

The management of the storeroom is in the hands of a housekeeper; she orders in the stores and gives them out as required; the house linen is in her charge, and it is her business to attend to it - to keep it in repair, and supply new when required; the china-closet is under her charge, and the stillroom department is superintended by her; she superintends the arrangements of the bedrooms, and both those for visitors and servants come under her daily supervision, and, subject to the approval of her mistress, she decides the rooms they are to occupy.

She requires to have methodical habits, to be firm and impartial in her dealings with the under servants, although strictly exacting respecting the due performance of their duties, as she in all respects represents her mistress, and is invested with her authority.

The daily round of a housekeeper's duties may be said to commence with her appearance in the housekeeper's room at half-past seven in the morning, when she proceeds to overlook the arrangements of the stillroom, to see that the china is given out for breakfast, together with the table-linen.

At eight o'clock she pours out the tea and presides over the housekeeper's-room breakfast, after which she again looks to the still-room arrangements for the family breakfast. She then gives out the stores for the day, and assists the stillroom maid to wash up the china in use, and puts the preserves away that have been on the breakfast-table; she then makes the round of the bedrooms, and sees that soap, candles, writing-paper, and inkstands have been attended to, and that the drawers and wardrobes have been properly dusted and papered; that the chintzes, muslin curtains, and covers are fresh, and that the rooms are thoroughly in order.

At one o'clock she leads the way into the servants' hall, and takes her place at the head of the dinner-table, and carves one of the joints; she then leads the way to housekeeper's-room, and takes the head of the table, and helps the sweets or cheese. In the afternoon she arranges the dessert for the dinner, and makes the tea for the drawing-room five o'clock tea. She also makes the coffee sent in after dinner. She sees that the dessert is put away when brought from the dining-room.

She makes the preserves and bottles the fruit; she is referred to respecting all domestic arrangements; she keeps the housekeeping accounts, and the greater part of the needlework required in the house is done by her, with or without assistance, according to the amount of work to be got through.

A very general plan, even in wealthy families, is for the cook to take the office of housekeeper, or even for the lady's-maid to do so.

In these cases the authority invested in their hands is not nearly so great as that invested in the hands of a housekeeper proper, and they may always be looked upon as deputy housekeepers, as the engaging and dismissing of the servants, the ordering of stores, and the active supervision of the household, still remain with the mistress; but in all other respects the duties are the same, although in some households the upper housemaid has the charge of the house and table-linen.

In the country the housekeeper materially helps her mistress in her charities to the poor, carries out her orders, and attends to her wants.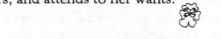

THE DUTIES OF A COOK

The duties of a cook depend greatly upon the scale of establishment to which she belongs. In the case of a professed cook the elementary portion of the cooking, the plain cooking, and all that relates to cleaning and scouring in the kitchen, scullery, larder, and passages and all cooking utensils, is done by the kitchen and scullery maids, and only the cooking proper is the duty of this class of cook. All ingredients are prepared for her use, and the kitchen-maids wait upon her and act under her orders.

A man cook takes even a higher position, and undertakes still less of the plain cooking of the house than does a woman cook.

A first-class cook is not expected to be down until a few minutes before eight, in time for breakfast in the steward's room or housekeeper's room. If she is housekeeper as well as cook, she makes and pours out the tea for the upper servants.

After her own breakfast, she attends to and super-intends the breakfast for the family, and the management of the breakfast is left in her hands, to provide what she judges best according to her knowledge of the style of breakfast that the family prefer. She makes out a menu for the day's dinner and for the day's luncheon on a slate according to the contents of the larder, and with due regard to variety. In some households the servants'-hall dinner is also written on a slate; in others it is left to the management of the cook.

Some mistresses have the slate brought to them by a footman at about eleven o'clock, and make any alteration they may think proper, and return it by him to the cook. Other mistresses have the slate brought to them by the cook, in place of having it sent up, and consult with him or her respecting any changes to the menu for the day. This is the most practical mode of proceeding, as, if the mistress has any suggestions to make in this direction, she can urge them upon the cook, or if she has a remark to offer, or a fault to find with the cook's mode of serving any particular dish, the opportunity is given for so doing.

Some ladies stand very much in awe of their cooks,

knowing that those who consider themselves to be thoroughly experienced will not brook fault-finding, or interference with the manner of cooking, and give notice to leave on the smallest pretext. Thus, when ladies obtain a really good cook, they deal with her delicately, and are inclined to let her have her own way with regard to serving the dinner.

Other ladies, again, who keep a professed cook, consider that all responsibility is thus taken off their hands, and do not trouble themselves to see the cook respecting the arrangements for the day, but leave them entirely to her discretion, and scarcely doing more than to glance at the menu. But, however high the capabilities of a cook, the relations between her and her mistress are on a much more satisfactory footing if she confers with her each morning, instead of merely approving the menu.

In town, the cook gives the necessary orders to the tradespeople who serve the house. If she is house-keeper and cook she gives out the stores required; she then prepares the soup for the following day, as soup is seldom made the day it is required to be eaten; the pastry, the jellies, the creams, the entrées are all made by her during the morning, and any dishes of this nature that are to be served at luncheon are also made by her. After her own dinner, she dishes up the luncheon. The servants'-hall dinner is cooked by the kitchen-maid.

The afternoon is very much at the cook's disposal, except on the occasion of a dinner party, or when guests are staying in the house, when there is naturally more work to be done. Five to nine always a very busy time with the cook; dishing up a large dinner is an arduous duty, the greatest order and regularity being maintained in the kitchen the while, perfect silence is enjoined save when an order is given concerning the work in hand. It would be an advantage if, in small establishments, this rule of silence was as absolute, as where gossiping in the kitchen is encouraged by the cook, hindrance and consequent delay in the work is the natural result.

When the dinner has been duly served the cook's duties for the day are over, and the remainder of the kitchen work is performed by the kitchen-maids.

In households where three are kept in the kitchen, cook, kitchen-maid, scullery-maid, the cook is less of an *artiste*, and more of the general cooking falls to her share, she having but one kitchen-maid to assist her; and where but one kitchen-maid is kept she does not undertake so much of the cooking as where two are kept; the head kitchen-maid in large establishments being practically a second cook.

In households where only two are kept in the kitchen, viz., cook and kitchen-maid, the cook unites the duties of head kitchen-maid to those of cook, while the kitchen-maid performs those of kitchen-maid and scullery-maid. This is a very large class of households, and here the mistress personally superintends things. Instead of the menu being prepared for her inspection, she herself inspects the contents of the larder attended by the cook; she makes her own suggestions as to what she will have for dinner and luncheon, and for the servants'-hall dinner, and writes down her orders for the cook to carry out.

Cooks in this class of household are expected to be down by seven o'clock and although they have not to light fires, or perform any cleaning and scouring of kitchen and basement, they are required to see that the kitchen-maid performs her duty in a thorough manner.

If the cook acts as housekeeper also, she makes and pours the tea in the housekeeper's room, and gives out the stores; she gives the necessary orders for the day to the tradespeople who send round for them, she cooks the luncheon and the servants' dinner, she cooks the family dinner, and she takes charge of all that is left from the dining-room dinner.

It is an understood thing that the cook has certain perquisites connected with her place, amongst others the dripping from the roast joints, of which, in large establishments, there is a considerable quantity. Economical mistresses will be glad if this large waste could be brought into use in the kitchen for frying and other purposes; but cooks absolutely refuse to comply with this wish, on the ground that it is their lawful perquisite! Noblemen with small means and gentlemen with small means are under the necessity of practising economy in every department of their households; and in these days of general retrenchment, when the mistress of a house curtails all household expenses in her power; to "keep down" the household bills is one of the first points of attack, and the kitchen offers a large field for such operations.

If a mistress is desirous of obtaining the co-operation of a cook in reducing expense in the kitchen, a little present made to her, will, in almost all cases, render her very amenable to any plan of this kind her mistress may propose; and there are many such points where a saving of expense can be arrived at without any falling off in the comfort of housekeeping.

In small households where only a cook is kept, with a scullery-maid, or a girl in the scullery, under her to do the rough work, her duties are many and heavy if the family is a large one, and if there is a great deal of cooking; but if the family is a small one, the contrary is the case. No responsibility as regards ordering or arranging for the meals of the house rests with her: though, if she is conscientious and careful of the interests of the family, she can materially assist her mistress in suggesting dishes, with a view to using the cold meat, &c., or in making suggestions for the servants' dinner, in accordance with the contents of the larder.

A mistress of a house expects to find the kitchen and all connected with it in perfect order by the time she is ready to order dinner; and a cook who unites method with cleanliness - two points of paramount importance in a cook - always keeps the kitchen in order.

A plain cook in a small household where no kitchen or scullery-maid is kept, also acts as parlour-maid, has other duties to perform unconnected with the kitchen. Her business is, then, to sweep and dust the dining-room, clean the grate, and light the fire; to sweep and clean the front hall and the front door-steps in addition to the work of the kitchen.

This class of cook is expected to be down as six in the summer and half-past six in the winter, and she lights the kitchen fire and gets through her work upstairs before putting her kitchen in order; she then lays the kitchen breakfast. After her own breakfast she cooks the breakfast for the family, she assists the housemaid to make her mistress's bed, and she answers the door up to half-past twelve.

Plain cooking makes but very little work in comparison with professed cooking. Copper stew-pans, sauté pans, a hot stove, a charcoal fire, a hot plate, a gas stove, are not in every-day use; and, oftener than not, the cook has a kitchener instead of a range to cook at; while the dinner generally consists of fish, a joint and vegetables, a pudding or tart; and the luncheon is either a joint, vegetables and plain pudding, or cold meant, salad and potatoes.

Ladies in search of a moderately good cook, and not willing to pay the high wages asked by a professed cook, generally find that a young woman who has been head kitchen-maid under a good cook, is far preferable to one who has been plain cook in a small family. A kitchen-maid has assisted in the best style of cooking, and has served her apprenticeship in a good school, she has had a great deal of practice in the first, second, and third principles of cooking, she knows how things ought to be done, and how they should taste, and how they should look. She is not so extravagant in her notions and ideas as is a professed cook, she is not so impatient of interference from her mistress, and is inclined to fall in with the ways of the house.

Plain cooks in small families are rarely those who have learnt the art of cooking in large households, but are in a great measure self-taught, and have often as much to unlearn as to learn.

Housekeeping arrangements in small households differ materially, thus influencing the work of the kitchen.

In some households the family have a hot joint for luncheon, with vegetables; this answers for luncheon in the dinning-room, for the children's dinner, and for the servants' dinner, therefore only one mid-day meal has to be cooked, but it is served differently according to the rules of the house. It is either sent up into the dining-room where the children dine at the family luncheon, and is then sent down for the servants' dinner; or the children's dinner is helped from the dining-room, slices of meat being placed upon a dish, and dishes of vegetables sent with it to the nursery or school-room, or the cook carves the joint in the kitchen, and sends up a dish of meat to the dining-room and one to the nursery. But this plan is only followed when but one or two members of the family are at home to luncheon. Again, there are households where there is a separate dinner for the servants: perhaps hot meat one day and cold meat another day, quite distinct from what is ordered for the dining-room, which luncheon consists of little dishes, rechauffés from the pervious night's dinner. This last method, although more economical, makes more work for the cook, and more scullery-work to be done.

The early part of the afternoon is required by her for this scullery-work. She has then to prepare the dining-room dinner, which, in this description of household, is served either at half-past six or seven. Where there is a house-maid kept as well as a parlour-maid, she assists the cook in dishing-up the dinner, but where the house-maid acts as parlour-maid a cook dishes-up without assistance. A plain cook has the scullery-work to do after the dinner is sent up, and to lay the supper-table for the servants' supper in the kitchen, and afterwards to clear it away.

If the cook were to put off washing the dishes, plates, and cooking utensils until the following morning, it would not only be untidy and unmethodical, but it would be throwing a burden of too much work upon the next day.

It is also her duty to see that the doors and windows of the basement are fastened securely, that the kitchen fire has burnt low, and that the gas in the kitchen and passages is turned off before retiring for the night, from ten to half-past ten being the usual hour for so doing in households of this description.

THE DUTIES OF KITCHEN-MAIDS, SCULLERY-MAIDS AND STILLROOM-MAIDS

THE DUTIES OF A KITCHEN-MAID rather depend upon whether she is head kitchen-maid, or sole kitchen-maid.

In large households kitchen-maids and a scullery-maid are usually kept, in which case the head kitchen-maid is almost an under-cook: she does all the plain cooking of the establishment, for the schoolroom, nursery, servants' hall, and housekeepers' room, besides much of the elementary cooking for the dining-room. She makes the sauces for the various courses, and prepares the different dishes under the directions of the cook.

The second kitchen-maid prepares the vegetables for the house, the game and the poultry; in some houses she does the dairy-work. She makes the bread if the head kitchen-maid has other work to do.

Where a stillroom-maid is not kept, the head kitchen-maid makes the cakes for luncheon, tea, and dessert, and makes the rolls for breakfast. The second kitchen-maid keeps the kitchen clean, scours the tables and keeps things in order where a servants'-hall boy is not kept. The second kitchen-maid lays the servants' meals in the servants' hall.

Where only one kitchen-maid is kept, she does less cooking and more of the kitchen-work: she assists the cook in preparing all the ingredients for her use; she makes the sauces; she cooks the servants' dinner; she bakes the bread; she prepares the vegetables and cooks them; she cleans the kitchen and lights the kitchen fire.

THE SCULLERY-MAID'S chief duty is to clean and scour the stewpans, saucepans, sauté pans, and all the utensils of the kitchen; to clean the scullery, servants' hall, larders, and kitchen passages; and where only one kitchen-maid is kept, it is the scullery-maid's duty to lay the table in the servants' hall for the servants' meals. The scullery-maid usually dines in the kitchen with the kitchen-maid, and attends meanwhile to the cooking that is going on for the family luncheon, during the absence of the cook in the servants' hall.

Kitchen-maids and scullery-maids are expected to rise at six o'clock in summer, and half-past six in winter.

In small households, where only two are kept in the kitchen, viz., a cook and a scullery-maid, the scullery-maid performs many of the duties of a kitchen-maid; she cleans the kitchen, lights the kitchen fire, prepares and cooks vegetables, assists the cook in the plain cooking, in addition to the scullery work, which is considerably lighter in small households than in large ones.

A vegetable maid is oftener kept in a club than in a private household, and her duty consists in preparing the vegetables for cooking.

In those establishments where large parties of visitors are constantly entertained, two stillroom-maids are often kept, and the stillroooom work is shared between them.

AMONGST THE MANY DUTIES OF THE STILLROOM-MAID are the following: to lay the housekeeper's-room breakfast-table, to bring in the breakfast, to clear away and wash up the breakfast things. To prepare the various trays for the eight o'clock bedroom teas. A small tea-tray is covered with a serviette, a cup of tea with a small milk-jug and sugar-basin, and plate with slices of bread and butter, are placed upon it. The tea is either made by the housekeeper or by the stillroom-maid. She also makes the rolls for breakfast, and gives out the china for the dining-room breakfast, and subsequently washes and puts it away. She waits in the housekeeper's-room, lays the cloth for dinner, and clears the dinner-table. She prepares the dessert dishes in readiness for the dessert. She gives out the china and cake for the drawing-room five o'clock tea. She prepares the housekeeper's-room tea, clears away the tea-things, washes and puts them away. She prepares the tray with the tea-cups and coffee-cups for the after dinner tea and coffee. She lays the house-keeper's-room supper-table, waits at supper, and clears the supper-table.

She is expected to rise at six o'clock to clean and sweep the housekeeper's-room and stillroom, to light the fires, and to assist the housekeeper in all that appertains to the housekeeper's-room duties.

HOUSEMAIDS' DUTIES

The duties of a housemaid depend in a great measure upon the scale of the household to which she belongs, and according to the number of housemaids kept - whether there are three housemaids or one housemaid, whether the duties are divided between three, or devolve upon one; and when they are divided between three - that is, between the upper and under-housemaids - the duties of the upper-housemaid are comparatively light as regards labour, but heavy as regards responsibility; the under-housemaids being under her supervision.

An upper-housemaid's duty is to take charge of the house-linen; to keep it in repair, and give it out as required; to see that each bedroom is supplied with clean chintzes, curtains, sofa-covers, chair-covers, toilet-covers, &c.; to see that the drawers and ward-robes are dusted and papered, and that fresh candles are set up each evening, soap supplied, writing-tables attended to, &c.

Her duty is also to dust the china ornaments in the drawing-rooms and other sitting-rooms, attend to the arrangements of the rooms, and to attend to the flowers and plants. The sitting-room, chintzes, and chair-covers, are also under her charge, when a house-deeper is not kept. She assists in making the beds in the best bedrooms, and in dusting the rooms and keeping everything in repair in each room.

After the dinner-bell has rung, she makes the round of the best bedrooms and dressing-rooms, to see that everything is in order, and that the under-housemaids have severally performed their duties.

When two housemaids are kept, the work of the household is divided between the two housemaids; although the upper-housemaid has the charge of the linen, and does the lighter work of the house.

When one housemaid is kept, she does not always have the charge of the house-linen, as it is sometimes given out by the mistress of the house, and sometimes by the lady's-maid; but she is expected to make out the list of linen when sent to a laundry, if not washed at home, and to see that it is correctly returned.

The arrangements of households where one housemaid is kept, differ considerably with regard to the work portioned to them.

The usual duties of a housemaid consist of the following: to rise at six in summer, and half-past six in winter; before breakfast to sweep and dust the drawing-room, dining-room, front hall, and other sitting-rooms; to clean the grates and light the fires; and where a lady's-maid or valet is not kept, she carries up the water for the baths for the family.

After her own breakfast she makes the servants' beds, sweeps, dusts, and arranges the rooms, sweeps the front staircase and front hall. She makes the best beds, and sweeps and dusts the rooms, cleans the grates, and lights the fires; when fires are kept up in the bedrooms during the day; it is her duty to attend to them, and to light them morning and evening, or when required; she prepares the bedrooms for the night, turns down the beds, fills the jugs with water, closes the curtains, takes up a can of hot water for the use of each person.

After the family have gone down to dinner, she again makes the round of the bedrooms, and puts them in order; her last duty being to take up a can of hot water to each bedroom and dressing room.

It is her duty to see, during the day, that each bedroom is supplied with soap, candles, clean towels, writing-paper, and all that is required for use.

In households where the housemaid acts as parlour-maid, the cook undertakes to sweep and dust the dining-room, to clean the grate and light the fire; to sweep and clean the front hall, and to clean the front doorsteps; and to assist in making the best beds.

Both sitting-rooms and bedrooms should be regularly swept and dusted each day; and the china fittings in bedrooms and dressing-rooms thoroughly cleaned.

Ill-trained housemaids are apt to neglect this daily round of sweeping and cleaning the rooms in use, and to postpone it until the end of the week.

This method of performing the house-work is not followed by good housemaids, or in well-regulated households.

An extra cleaning of each room once a month is necessary, independent of the attention and care that they require daily, when mirrors, pictures, windows, walls, &c., are cleaned, for which sufficient time cannot be allowed every morning.

A housemaid is expected to be dressed by four or half-past four in the afternoon, and to sit down to needlework.

When a housemaid acts as parlour-maid, she is required to be dressed before luncheon or the mid-day-diner, and to wear a clean cap and apron when bringing in the family breakfast.

When a housemaid acts as parlour-maid, she answers the door in the afternoon, and lays the table for dinner, &c.

Where two or three housemaids are kept, the upper and second housemaid are expected to do the needlework of the house in the afternoon - from three to five.

In small families, where one housemaid is kept, she undertakes to do the needlework for the house in the afternoon; and in many cases she is engaged to act as maid to her mistress, as regards assisting her in dressing.

THE DUTIES OF A PARLOUR-MAID

A large class of persons find it expedient to keep a parlour-maid rather than a man-servant; in watering-places, suburban towns, and even in town itself, persons with good incomes, but who live rather quietly prefer to be waited upon by a parlour-maid.

The wages of a parlour-maid are not so high as those of a man-servant, and there is a further saving in the matter of finding clothes, in addition to which the keep of a man-servant costs more than that of a female servant.

A parlour-maid lays the breakfast-table, takes in breakfast, but is not expected to wait at breakfast. She removes the breakfast-things, washes the china and silver, she lays the luncheon-table, carries in the luncheon, and waits at luncheon. She clears the luncheon-table, and washes the glasses and silver. She prepares the afternoon tea, carries it into the drawing-room, and afterwards removes it. She lays the table for dinner, and waits at dinner.

She waits upon her mistress; takes up her hot water, her morning cup of tea; assists her in dressing, and acts in every respect as lady's-maid with the exception of making her dresses; but she keeps the wardrobe of her mistress in order, and alters and repairs her dresses, &c., and does all necessary plain sewing. She does all the housemaid's work that relates to the drawing-room, sweeping, cleaning, and dusting the same. She cleans the silver, and has the charge of it. She cleans and trims all lamps that are used in the sitting-rooms. She gets up the fine linen of the ladies of the family. She does all pantry work, and keeps the pantry clean and in order. She opens the door to callers, both morning and afternoon. She is expected to be dressed by 1 o'clock p.m., in time to wait at luncheon, and to sit down to needlework not later than 2.30 p.m. She closes all shutters in hall, dining-room, library, and drawing-rooms before dinner, and lights the lamps or gas, or turns on the electric lights, in all sitting-rooms and corridors and hall as soon as it is dusk.

In the morning she wears a light cotton dress, apron, and cap; and a black merino dress, white bib apron and cap, collar and cuffs in the afternoon.

THE DUTIES OF LADY'S-MAID

There are various classes of ladies'-maids, - fine
maids and humble maids, clever maids, and maids
without any pretensions to cleverness; maids who are
their mistress's "right hand" as it were, coadjutors in
all that concerns the interest of the household; and
maids who are mere automatons, who perform the
duties required of them in a mechanical manner, and
who are more alive to their own interest than to that
of their mistress; maids who act as housekeeper, and
maids who act as nurse, first-class maids and second
class maids, experienced maids and inexperienced
maids, smart maids and maids who are not smart;
French maids and English maids.

A first-class maid is expected to be a thoroughly

experienced one: to be a first-rate hair-dresser and dressmaker, experienced in dressing a lady, and a good and expeditious packer, mistress of everything that appertains to her office. This description of maid is usually engaged by ladies who go out a "great deal," and who spend a considerable amount of money and time upon their dress.

These maids expect large perquisites in the matter of their mistress's wardrobes, and therefore seldom take a situation in what is termed a quiet family, where the mistress goes out but little and has not the reputation of being a good dresser.

This class of maid is often a Frenchwoman, and is only in her element in a large establishment, and households arranged on an economical footing do not meet the views of this order of lady's-maid; when engaged by the mistress of such, their stay is of the briefest, and too often fraught with annoyances and disagreeables to the household in general.

A Parisian maid out of her orbit is not a treasure
In her orbit, as attendant to an extravagant, wealthy and fashionable mistress, she suits the post, and what is no less important, the post suits her; but in engaging a Parisian maid, ladies find it necessary to be additionally cautious in their enquiries as to the character and to take little or nothing upon trust, or they may have

occasion to regret such credulity.

Swiss maids, on the contrary, are valuable acquisitions to a household on whatever scale it is regulated; they are not too grand in their ideas to suit the smallest establishment, and are generally sufficiently competent to undertake the duties of maid to the mistress of a large establishment.

They are, as a rule, trustworthy and solid, and the reverse of flighty in their conduct; they attach themselves with their interest; and although they may not posses the sparkling vivacity and style of the Parisian maid, they yet have sufficient tastes and skills and light handiness to fulfil all their duties in a thoroughly satisfactory manner.

A useful class of maid is the one who acts as housekeeper as well as maid; she is a good dressmaker, good hair-dresser, and what is known as a good maid. She undertakes as much dressmaking as the maid who does not act as housekeeper, and the fact of her being a deputy housekeeper places her more en rapport with her mistress than is the case with the generality of maids.

Ladies who consider themselves their own housekeepers place great reliance upon and trust in a maid occupying this position in a household.

All those who have any pretensions to the title of lady's-maid are expected thoroughly to understand the business of dressmaking, and not to possess merely a superficial knowledge of it, and the same with regard to hair-dressing and getting up fine linen.

The inexperienced, or humble maid, is but a novice in these essential points, and she asks comparatively low wages in consequence of this want of knowledge; but if unskilful when left to herself, she is at least expected to be a good workwoman, and to be able to carry out her mistress's instructions, and to work under her directions.

Young ladies' maids are generally of this order, though to this rule there are exceptions, as to every rule; and some ladies find it more advantageous to engage a first-class maid to wait upon their daughters, capable of accomplishing all the dressmaking that is required, in preference to a young and inexperienced maid with but an elementary knowledge of her duties.

Some ladies do not make a point of having much dressmaking done at home by their maid, and prefer having their dresses from a dressmaker, but to these ladies economy is presumably not an object.

Other ladies take, perhaps, a medium course, and have, on an average, two or three best dresses from a first-class dressmaker, and have their less expensive dresses made at home by their maid.

The duties of a maid may be said to consist of the following:-

To bring up the hot-water for her mistress in the morning and at various times of the day as required.

To bring her an early cup of tea.

To prepare her things for dressing.

To assist her in dressing.

To put her room in order after dressing.

To put out her things for walking, riding and driving, both in the morning and afternoon.

To assist her in taking off her out-door attire.

To put in readiness all that her mistress may require for dressing in the evening.

To assist her to dress for dinner.

To put everything in order in her mistress's room before leaving it.

To sit up for her, and to assist her to undress on her return, and to carefully put away her jewels and everything connected with her toilette.

To keep her mistress's wardrobe in thorough repair, and to do all the dressmaking and millinery required of her.

To wash the lace and fine linen of her mistress.

These are the ostensible duties of a lady's-maid, but there are many minor matters that in small households come within her province, such as dusting the china ornaments in the drawing-room, attending to the flowers in the drawing-room or in any of the sitting-rooms of the house.

When ladies keep a pet dog or dogs, it is the duty of a lady's-maid to attend to them; wash them, feed them, and take them out walking.

In small households where only one man-servant is kept, when he is out with the carriage in the afternoon, the lady's-maid undertakes to answer the door to visitors, and in still smaller households where the housemaid undertakes the parlour work, the lady's-maid answers the door until the luncheon hour; but whenever these exceptional arrangements are made, it is necessary to mention them at the time of engaging a lady's-maid, thus giving her the option of refusing to undertake a situation where these extra duties are required of her.

In some small households the nurse acts as lady's-maid to her mistress, in so far as rendering her assistance in dressing and keeping her wardrobe in order.

With regard to the perquisites of ladies'-maids, the apparel that a mistress has left off wearing is given to the lady's-maid and considered to be perquisite, but some ladies make an exception to this rule with regard to their more expensive dresses, while others make an exception in favour of all their apparel, for diverse reasons; one reason being an objection to seeing their maids wearing dresses that they themselves have recently worn, while other ladies prefer giving away their discarded dresses to poor relations for the use of their families.

On the death of a mistress, the lady's-maid in her service usually claims the wardrobe, with the exception of lace, fur, velvet, and satin, unless an arrangement has been made of the nature above alluded to.

The leisure accorded to ladies' maids consists principally of the evening hours, from eight o'clock until bedtime; but mistresses are, as a rule, very indulgent in allowing their maids to walk out in the afternoon if they desire to do so, and to attend church twice on Sunday, whole holidays being, as a rule, more or less inconvenient to grant.

A sewing-maid does needlework and dress-making only, and does not wait upon the ladies of the family unless specially engaged to do so.

THE DUTIES OF A HEAD-NURSE AND A NURSERY-MAID

THE DUTIES OF A NURSE, although comparatively light, are yet weighted with heavy responsibility, the office of nurse being one in which great trust is reposed, and much confidence placed.

To secure a nurse in whom all requisite qualities for the situation are united, is a matter of no little difficulty; good qualities are too often negatived by serious defects of character, and although the moral points in the character of a nurse may be excellent, and the knowledge of the duties of her position complete, yet these advantages are more frequently counterbalanced by some serious fault, such as undue impulsiveness in the management of children. This impulsiveness springs probably from an undisciplined mind, is the attribute of the class to which they belong!

A hasty temper, over which but little or no restraint has been exercised; from which springs the ill-judged punishing, and ill-timed spoiling which are distinguishing characteristics of many head-nurses of the day.

A love of gossiping with their fellow-servants in the presence of the children themselves; their vulgarisms of speech, and the topics discussed by them totally unfitted for the ears of children; are but a few of the numerous failings of those who might otherwise by justly considered good nurses.

The diction of a nurse is also of serious importance to the children under her care. If she is an uneducated woman, she mispronounces and miscalls almost every word she utters, and the children, with all the quickness of childhood, contract habits of speech which are subsequently difficult to overcome. Others, again, display a great disregard for the letter H, or perhaps a misplaced affection for it; and although it may amuse the members of the family when she talks of "*Master 'Enery's beautiful blue heyes*," it is not perhaps quite so amusing when Master Henry himself informs his mamma's visitor that he has "'*urt his 'ead*" and "*pinched his 'and.*"

In contrast to this Cockney dialect so often met with in nurses, is the broad dialect of the labouring classes, from which classes nurses are most frequently taken; they enter families as nursery-maids, and their uneducated dialect is not supposed to signify, but in the course of years, when they are promoted to the post of head-nurse, it signifies materially.

Mothers are too often induced to overlook this serious defect on the part of a nurse, on account of her other many excellent qualities, believing, moreover, that a governess, when the children are old enough to require one, will very easily eradicate any uncouthness of speech contracted by them in the nursery. How fallacious is this impression, those who have in childhood been under the care of an uneducated nurse bear unpleasing testimony.

Children are prone to copy and to take impressions from those with whom their infantine days are spent; and as it is their nurse with whom these days are passed, they derive all their impressions from her, if they are not living photographs of her; her violence of temper is reproduced in them with startling fidelity, and act of duplicity or underhand manoeuvring is noted, remembered, and acted upon, on the first occasion, and untruthfulness in children, if traced to its origin, would often be found to have originated in an untruthful nurse. It is so with all the moral qualities, every bad quality in the nurse is reproduced in children with painful accuracy.

The nursery is oftener than not the children's world; their mother is to them the beautiful lady whom they see ten minutes during the day, and whose visits to the nursery are of the briefest; when this is so, the influence of the nurse is supreme over the minds of her charges.

Even when mothers pass such of their time with their children, having them frequently with them, and endeavouring to counteract the nurse's influence, yet from the position the nurse holds toward them, and from the nature of her duties, it naturally follows that her example and authority are paramount with them. Thus the character and the daily life of the nurse are instinct with teaching, in comparison with which the precepts and instructions of parents weigh but slightly in the balance.

The manner and bearing of nurses towards children has also its effect upon them; children become brusque, abrupt in their speech, in proportion as the nurse is or is not so in these things.

Vulgarisms of speech taught by a nurse, can, by constant care, be counteracted and corrected by a governess or mother; but a broad country dialect, once acquired, clings to a child, and gives a very disagreeable twang to the voice, which no after-instruction can remedy.

Mothers awake to the responsibility attached to

the choice of a nurse, bear these drawbacks and disadvantages well in mind, when selecting one for their children; while less experienced mothers make every allowance for shortcomings imagining that, as the children are so young, constant contact with an uneducated person leaves no lasting impression or ill effects upon their characters.

More enlightened mothers, anxious for the early training of their children, unable to meet with a nurse who comes up in any degree to their standard of excellence, have recourse to the expedient of engaging young-lady nurses or widow ladies, to act in this capacity.

When young-lady nurses are selected, they are taken from large families of daughters, well brought-up girls, accustomed to assist their mothers in the management of their brothers and sisters, and thus experienced with the ways of childhood.

The position these young-lady nurses hold in household is that of nursery-governesses; they have breakfast and tea in the nursery, they dine down at the family luncheon, and supper is sent to them in the nursery.

They perform all the duties of a nurse, taking charge of an infant from a month old; the maternal instinct which is inherent in every woman is not by any means the prerogative of uneducated classes, quite the contrary; and all hygienic and sanitary principles which can be introduced and carried out in the nursery are far better understood and put into practice by intelligent and educated women, than by obstinate uneducated ones, in whom prejudice too often usurps the place of common sense.

Children placed in the charge of a well-brought-up, well-mannered, high-principled young woman, are not exposed to the coarse and rough jests which are too often indulged in by nurses and nursery-maids with the opposite sex in the presence of the children, and which have the most pernicious effect upon their young minds, rendering them over precocious, and versed in vulgar street-chaff; whereas, in the care of a lady-nurse, they are kept from such deteriorating influences.

The duties of a nurse are the same, whether they are performed by an uneducated or educated person; the rough work of the nursery is done by the nursery-maid.

When the nurse has the charge of more than one child, the nursery-maid assists her in washing and dressing the elder children; when there is only one child in her care, she has no assistance from a nursery-maid or housemaid, as in such a case the under-housemaid waits upon the nursery, a nursery-maid not being considered necessary.

A nurse is not supposed rise later than seven; at half-past seven the infant or child has its bath, and is then dressed; eight o'clock is the breakfast hour, which is prepared by the nursery or housemaid.

At half-past nine in summer, and eleven in winter, the children are taken out; if there are two children or more, the nursery-maid accompanies the nurse in the walk.

At twelve o'clock the young children are made to lie down for at least an hour; one o'clock is the nursery dinner-hour, but in the case of a lady-nurse, she dines with family at their luncheon.

At half-past two the children are again taken out, weather permitting, for an hour or an hour and a half; at half-past four the nurse is probably desired to bring the children to the drawing-room, and there to leave them with their mother, for from twenty minutes to half an hour.

Sometimes the children are brought down after instead of before tea, five o'clock being the hour for nursery-tea; but as half-past five is near to the hour of young children's bed-time, they are rather inclined to be cross and sleepy if taken to the drawing-room after they have had their tea.

Six o'clock is the usual hour for children to retire to rest. The evening bath is prepared by the nursery-maid, as is the morning bath.

Supper is brought to the nurse in the nursery at half-past eight or nine o'clock. In some households she has dinner and supper with the other servants, while in others she has all her meals in the nursery, which are brought to her by the nursery-maid or under-housemaid. Mistresses find that the latter is the better plan to follow.

A nurse is expected to cut out and make the children's ordinary under-clothing; some nurses are not capable of doing even this with any degree of satisfaction to their mistresses, and are only equal to keeping the children's garments in repair, and making the plainest under-clothing.

Children's dresses, pinafores, and petticoats, are now made in so elaborate a style, that a nurse had need to be a clever dressmaker to attempt to make frocks for the children, and this accomplishment is not expected of them.

After supper a nurse's time is her own as regards needlework, although she is required to remain in the day-nursery within call if wanted. a nurse is allowed to attend church once every Sunday, and to go out one evening in each week, and in every month or six weeks she is allowed one whole day or half day, according to the arrangements made between herself and mistress at the time of engaging her.

Although going out without leave is not permitted

in well-regulated households, yet should the nurse venture upon doing so, it is looked upon as a graver offence on her part than on that of any other servant by reason of the responsibility of her position.

On the other hand, mistresses are more considerate and more indulgent to their nurses than to any other servant in the establishment, in many instances humouring them and spoiling them, with the idea of attaching them to the children under her charge. The result of this system is that the nurse presumes upon the weakness of her mistress and becomes tyrannical and overbearing, and impatient of control and interference.

Occasionally a mistress of a family is fortunate enough to meet with a nurse who is exempt from the drawbacks enumerated, and who is all that a nurse should be; but these exceptional women are difficult to meet with, and the majority of nurses belong to the order before described rather than to this superior and exceptional type of nurse.

THE NURSERY-MAID'S DUTIES. - The nursery-maid's duties are of a very practical and subordinate character. She has but to execute the orders of the nurse, and to do all that is required of her in a thorough manner. She is expected to rise at six o'clock, to sweep and dust the day nursery, clean the grate, and light the fire; to light the fire in the night nursery when one is required; to bring up the water for the children's baths; to assist the nurse in washing and dressing the children; to lay the nursery breakfast-table; and afterwards to clear away and wash up the breakfast things; to make the beds and empty the baths; to sweep and clean the night nursery; to accompany the children out walking in the morning, or to be ready to sit down to needle-work for the children if she remains at home; to assist in undressing the children, and to put their walking things away; to set the nursery dinner-table, and to bring up and clear away the nursery dinner, including that of the nurse and her own; to go out with the children in the afternoon, if required, or to do needle-work if not required to go out; to play with and amuse the children before tea; to prepare the nursery tea for the children, nurse, and herself, and to wash up and put away the tea-things; to prepare the children's evening baths and to assist in undressing, washing, and putting them to bed; to assist the nurse in preparing the children's things for wear the next morning; to bring up the supper for the nurse and herself.

After this meal her time is at her own disposal for the remainder of the evening.

THE DUTIES OF
DAIRY-MAIDS AND LAUNDRY-MAIDS

THE DIARY-MAID is sometimes an outdoor servant, and sometimes an indoor servant; it depends in a great measure whether the dairy is a large or small one; if a large one, the dairy-maid usually lives at the home-farm, and churns the butter, and looks after the poultry - milking the cows being done by the stock-man.

The combined duties of attending to the poultry and to the work of the dairy are sometimes performed by two dairy-maids, and sometimes by one, according to the amount of poultry or number of cows kept.

Rearing chickens, ducks, turkeys, &c., is a business in itself; and oftener than not, the stock-man assists the dairy-maid in churning, when there is a considerable amount of butter to be made.

When the dairy-maid is an indoor servant, she is kitchen-maid as well as dairy-maid, and the dairy work is comparatively light; extra wages are given when these combined duties are undertaken by her.

A LAUNDRY-MAID is also a semi-outdoor servant, although she has her meals in the servant's hall, and lives in the house; but the laundry is usually a de-tached building.

Where two or three laundry-maids are kept, the upper laundry-maid attends to getting up the fine linen for the family and the under laundry-maids to the house linen and servant's linen; but in small country establishments, where only one laundry-maid is kept, the under servants are expected to give a couple of hours of their time during the week, to assist in ironing their own cotton dresses. In other small establishments where resident laundry-maids are not kept, laundry-maids from the neighbouring village are hired by the week; but are boarded in the house with the other servants.

In towns the washing of the family in a household is put out, and is either paid for by the piece, dozen, or by contract.

THE DUTIES OF
GARDENERS AND GAMEKEEPERS

A HEAD GARDENER in a large establishment is an individual of no little importance, and is usually a man possessing a considerable amount of practical knowledge and a fair education; there is generally a great deal of glass under his charge, hot-houses, green-houses, conservatories, &c.

Some gardeners direct much of their attention and skill to forcing fruit, flowers, and vegetables, and are allowed by their masters to exhibit specimens of their skill in this direction, but as this forcing system, when carried out to any extent, is attended with no little expense, both as regards money and time, some masters object to its being indulged in; and again, many people think that moderate forcing, for their own table, of such vegetables as potatoes, French beans, peas, asparagus, in addition to cucumbers and mush-rooms, &c., are all that is required, and dispense with such luxuries as strawberries, pines, and melons until they are fairly in season and not wholly out of season.

The number of gardeners kept, in addition to the head gardener, is regulated by the size of the gardens and extent of the operations carried on; but it is the head gardener's duty to apportion the work to each man employed in the gardens and to see that it is properly performed; he is rather an autocrat in his way, and is usually studied and conciliated by the feminine branches of the family.

He objects, on principle, to his choicest blooms being cut by his mistress or her daughters, or the finest bunches of grapes being gathered; when his green-houses and hot-houses are to be rifled, he prefers that is should be done by himself rather than by his mistress, and ladies who value their gardeners are inclined to humour this weakness.

The scale of gardeners varies as much as the extent of the gardens themselves, from the gardens of a castle to those of a cottage or villa; from the head gardener, with twenty-five gardeners under him, to the one gardener who is assisted in his labours by a boy, or is even unassisted by a boy, and who adds to his duty of gardener that of groom, taking charge of pony and pony-carriage.

THE DUTIES OF A GAMEKEEPER hardly come within the province of the present work.

The wages a gamekeeper receives are mentioned in the tariff of servant's wages.

The head gamekeeper occupies a cottage on the estate, and the second keeper is provided with a cottage also; the head keeper attends to preserving game, rearing pheasants, and so on, and has the management of the manor, subject to his master's approval, and of the battues, or shooting parties; the under-keepers receive the instructions from him.

CONCLUDING REMARKS

The treatment of servants by masters and mistresses greatly influences the services rendered; considerate masters and mistresses usually obtain good service from their domestics, and consideration is best shown by as far as possible not interrupting them in the performance of their duties, thus allowing of their being carried out with method and regularity.

Again, inexperienced mistresses make the mistake of being over confidential with their servants at one hour, and expecting them to be over deferential the next. They are confidential respecting their own affairs, which provokes a corresponding degree of confidence on the part of their servants, good mistresses take an interest in the welfare and well-being of their servants; and thus gain an influence over them for good; but this is a very different thing to encouraging them in idle gossip, as a servant once permitted to become a narrator too often draws the long bow, and fact is lost in fiction.

On the other hand, some masters and mistresses adopt an arbitrary and haughty demeanour towards their servants, to the exclusion of anything like a mutual interest, such as it is well should exist between masters and servants.

Servants should neither be treated in a too conciliatory manner nor in a too peremptory one, and a manner and bearing bordering on neither of these extremes is calculated to inspire the greatest amount of respect and obedience. A hesitating manner when giving an order of however trivial a nature, or an appeal to the judgement of a servant as to whether an order given is the best to give under the circumstances, renders it liable to be disregarded and set on one side altogether, or carelessly and indifferently executed - as servants as a rule are quick to take advantage of any weakness of character or purpose exhibited by their masters and mistresses.

THE END.

Other Copper Beech Gift Books for you to collect include:-

How To Entertain Your Guests
A book of traditional indoor games collected in 1911. A companion book to 'The Duties of Servants'

Mangles Mops & Feather Brushes
Advice for the laundry and spring cleaning the old-fashioned way

Etiquette for Gentlemen
Rules for perfect behaviour for the gentleman in every woman's life

Poetry Thoughts & Merry Jests
Words of friendship from Victorian and Edwardian autograph albums

Love is like a Mutton Chop...
Wry words of love 1840-1940

A Mother holds you by the heart...
A book of treasured wordsfor Mother

Grandma
..a grandchild I love for company, some tea a cat and a book...
This book will delight grandmothers any time of the year

The Ladies Oracle
Reveal your destiny by consulting this oracle devised in 1857.

For a free catalogue write to
Copper Beech Publishing Ltd,
PO Box 159, East Grinstead, Sussex, RH19 4FS, England

126

A CIP catalogue record for this book is available from the
British Library

Line illustrations used courtesy of Mike Banwell, Baskerville Books,
Tunbridge Wells.

Thanks to Jan and Graham Upton at 'How We Lived Then' Museum
of Shops Eastbourne for permission to photograph their collection of
Victorian household objects.

Photography by Allen Barnes

Cover design by Angela Morgan

Printed and bound in Great Britain

Copper Beech Gift Books
are designed and printed in the
United Kingdom